Webster's Tea Time Guest

By
Catherine Richardson

Dedication

To George,Noah and Milly. You have been the inspiration since day one.

Acknowledgement

Dad, I wouldn't be who I am without you. Unfortunately Dementia has stolen you from us. I wish you could have been present to see this and be proud.

About the Author

Kate Richardson born in Ipswich Suffolk, now resides in Oxford and works as a Biomedical Scientist for the NHS

One sunny morning in the middle of spring

Webster the spider began to spin

He spun and he spun until it was done

Then whistled with joy in the midday sun

He sat for a snack and he thought for a while

How nice it would be to show his home off in style

But who should he invite? What could they have for tea?

Then he wondered whether his friend Greg might be free?

Greg was an aphid, as green as green can be

Some call him a greenfly, he's the gardener's' enemy

He doesn't mean to be a pest, to be good is his aim

But it isn't easy when you've only ever been a pain

Webster crawled over to the rose tree where Greg lived

And invited him to tea and cake

Which he promised he would make

Greg indeed was overjoyed at the thought of such a treat

That he straight away agreed to the offer to partake

They planned to meet at four "o" clock

At Webster's brand new shack

And Greg was carried up to it upon the spiders back

They settled down to drink the tea and eat the cake prepared

When Webster up and ate his friend

As if he'd never cared

So if you are a small and green common garden pest

You might be wise to never be a spiders tea time guest.

www.ingramcontent.com/pod-product-compliance
Lightning Source LLC
Chambersburg PA
CBHW042146030726
47599CB00002B/638